thread

PAINTING

bunnies in my garden

First published in 2003 by

Sally Milner Publishing Pty Ltd
734 Woodville Rd
Binda NSW 2583
AUSTRALIA

© Jenny McWhinney 2003
Reprinted 2016

Design by Natalie Bowra
Editing by Gabrielle Canny
Illustrations by Jenny McWhinney
Stitch diagrams by Anna Warren
Photography by Tim Connolly

Printed in China

The National Library of Australia Cataloguing-in-Publication data:

McWhinney, Jenny.
Thread painting : bunnies in my garden.

ISBN 9 781863 514989

1. Embroidery – Patterns. I. Title. (Series : Milner craft series).

746.44

DISCLAIMER
The information in this instruction book is presented in good faith. However, no warranty is given, nor results guaranteed, nor is freedom from any patent to be inferred. Since we have no control over the use of information contained in this book, the publisher and the author disclaim liability for untoward results.

thread PAINTING

bunnies in my garden

Jenny McWhinney

SALLYMILNER
PUBLISHING

"Listen girls, I want to tell you something very exciting.
I had such a surprise this morning when I opened my back door...
I looked into my garden and couldn't believe my eyes, those dear little bunnies
had raked up all the leaves and mowed the lawn. They had left a basket of
freshly laid eggs and a little string bag full of crisp red apples..."

I dedicate this book to my loving husband, Ron and to our two wonderful daughters, Jessica and Sarah-Kate.

ACKNOWLEDGEMENTS

I wish to thank my entire family, from whom I get most of my inspiration, directly and indirectly; their love, enthusiasm and humour affects everything I do.

My friends also, who forgive me for not attending many organised lunches because of my stitching commitments. Even though I don't often attend, they never forget to invite me.
A very special thanks to friend and fellow designer, Sharon Venhoek, who assembled my twelve embroidered panels into the beautiful quilted wall hanging. Her excellent sewing skills have ensured my project has turned out exactly as I had pictured in my mind months before.

I would like to acknowledge Gumnut Yarns who supplied me with their magnificent threads and Rajmahal Threads for their superb Art silks.
Thankyou to Aussie Heirloom Mini Piping for their coloured piping, which so perfectly frames each of the bunny panels.

And finally, thankyou to Sally Milner Publishing for making a dream come true.

contents

inspiration

As a little girl, I travelled with my family to many exotic places. My father was in the Royal Air Force and we lived in North Africa, Aden, Singapore and many other beautiful places. I always remember the excitement of arriving in a new country, all the wonderful, different colours and smells; from the dusty plains of Africa with rich earthy colours, to the exciting Asian reds and golds.

I was constantly astounded at the differences in wildlife and vegetation of each place. One week I was living among the camels and sands of Aden, the next, among the English meadows and hedgerows alive with little hedgehogs and rabbits. My brothers and I were taught to embrace and learn from our exposure to different cultures and countries. This was a valuable lesson, carried with me through all aspects of my life.

I now live in Australia and love to recreate my memories through my sketching and stitching. During my early childhood, I loved drawing and painting the things I discovered. Stitching came at a later age. I was about thirteen years old when I realized there was a whole world of creating to be done with an embroidery needle. My early needlework projects involved simple stitches, really just 'colouring in' with threads, the creatures I had drawn. From there, I progressed to using a greater variety of stitches and threads, achieving a more sophisticated effect with stitch direction and colour.

For the last ten years I have created and taught needlework projects mostly in Adelaide, but also travelling to other cities around Australia. I enjoy the satisfaction of watching embroiderers fall in love with a design and progressing through a project to completion, using the simple techniques of thread painting. In this book I have set out all the instructions you will need to achieve just that.

I have called these projects, "Bunnies in my garden" because of the inspiration
that came from my very special Mum.
My two delightful daughters were born in 1988 and 1990, eighteen months apart.
As any mother would know, it gets a bit tricky when two tiny girls are both
being a little trying with tantrums and mini mood swings.

For me, help would come rushing in, in the form of my Mum, whose eyes would
open wide and she would say, "Oh girls, guess what the bunnies in my garden
have done."

She would take their attention and keep them occupied by telling them how she
had to make the bunnies porridge that morning before she came to visit, or how
one of the bunnies was naughty and dug up her roses.
The stories were endless and every one magical. Whether my girls were in a
supermarket trolley or in a car restraint, it worked like magic. Even when we
went to visit Mum and the girls asked to see the bunnies in her garden, there
was yet another story about the bunnies having just left to post a letter.

As the girls grew, they kept asking about the bunnies, even though they knew
they couldn't be true.

In my busy life I had forgotten about these tall tales, but was delighted when
Mum showed me a birthday card one of my daughters had sent her.
At the bottom it read:

"Thanks Nan, for the stories about the
bunnies in your garden."

thread painting

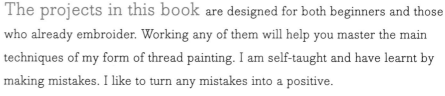

The projects in this book are designed for both beginners and those who already embroider. Working any of them will help you master the main techniques of my form of thread painting. I am self-taught and have learnt by making mistakes. I like to turn any mistakes into a positive.

I truly believe everyone is capable of so much more than they realize. Many times ladies come to my classes thinking they can only colour between the lines…not so! It is wonderful to see how, with a little confidence, they are able to relax and start to create in a more freehand style.

I hope to lower blood pressure not to raise it! My style of thread painting is very relaxed. I like to make the comparison that the difference between my style and that of traditional thread painting, is like the difference between folk art, with its disciplined strokes and the free spirit of watercolours.

Working these rabbits will help you to understand the reasons why a particular colour can change the shape of something or make it appear more realistic.

Another very important factor to remember is Mother Nature.

She did not create all rabbits (or any other plant, insect or animal for that matter) identical, so if your "*Mowing Bunny*" has slightly bigger feet than your "*Honey Bunny*", if your "*Autumn Bunny*" has fatter cheeks or whisker pads than "*Potting Bunny*", that's great! This gives each rabbit his or her own personality.

This principal works the same way for the flowers and foliage. Before you start to stitch, pick a bunch of roses or daisies from your garden, put them in a vase and spend some time seeing them, not just looking, but actually seeing them. Notice every rose or daisy is at its own particular stage of development, each one is a slightly different shade depending on which side of the bush it grew on and how much sunshine it received. Some petals may have been nibbled by aphids or caterpillars and a leaf may have been burnt by the morning frost.

As with daisies and roses, examine the sleeve of the blouse, dress, jacket or trousers you are wearing. Look at other peoples clothing, notice the creases in the sleeves, folds in the lapels and how stripes disappear in these folds. This is

My style of
thread painting
is very relaxed

how you need to embroider. I have shown examples of this in "Autumn Bunny".
Don't try to keep things perfectly straight unless you are working on something
like a broom handle or a window ledge.

When you look at your stitching in a more realistic and forgiving way, you will
become a more creative person. It is the imperfections, as well as the
perfections, of Mother Nature, that makes her so wonderful.

UNDERSTANDING YOUR SUBJECT

To understand the simple anatomy or shape to be stitched, pay close attention to
your subject. For example, a rabbit's eyes are of a medium to large size for it's
body size, and they are quite bulbous. This is why, in some of these bunnies,
depending on the angle at which they are standing, you can still see a little of
the eye of the far side. This would not be the case with a guinea pig or rat as
their eyes are smaller and not so bulbous.

OUTLINING

The way you outline is very important. I don't like the unnatural look of a thick
outline, it is better to just emphasise the area stitched. For example it is better to
emphasise the hem or edge of a jacket, rather then encircle the entire jacket.

SIMPLICITY

I always try to keep things simple. Most of my work is embroidered in a basic
stitch. I give the subject I am working on shape and texture by the colour and
type of thread I use. I don't believe it is the number of different stitches you use,
but how you use them.

Once you have mastered the simple technique of interlocked straight stitch and
recognise stitch direction, you will really come to love thread painting.

I warn you that once you have become hooked, it pays to teach the family to
cook their own dinner!

*dummy caption observing
your subject closely*

thread painting

DIAGRAM A

DIAGRAM B

DIAGRAM C

INTERLOCKED STRAIGHT STITCH

I work mostly with this method because it is so versatile. Think of your needle as a paintbrush.

The stitches should be kept between 6mm (²/8″) and 9mm (³/8″) long, depending on the project or shape of the area you are working on. For example, if you were embroidering a frog, when stitching the head and body, your stitches would be approximately 9mm (³/8″) long, but when working the little toes, you would reduce the length to 6mm (²/8″) or a little less. This is also the case when working around a corner, for example an elbow or a heel.

If the stitches become too long, they are more likely to catch when the item is complete. Don't work in rows as is often shown in examples of interlocked long and short stitch. If you work this way ridges can appear.

When I want to create a smooth surface, as for a ballerina's leotard or for skin, I work the stitches by putting the needle in between other stitches worked rather than piercing them. I also put the needle in the fabric at about a 40-degree angle. If I wish to stitch a fuzzy bear or a tweed coat, I pierce the stitches already laid down and do not concern myself about the angle of the needle.

STITCH DIRECTION

Recognising stitch direction is very important. Although not always obvious, it gives the work dimension and texture. Pay very close attention to each project's stitch direction chart. Think of a current in a river or the grooves you make in sand or soil with a rake.

When learning to achieve good stitch direction this hint will make it easy. Using the thread you are about to work with, for example if working *Cauliflower Bunny's* jacket, put in a few stitch direction lines as shown in diagram A. Then work in between these lines, always keeping your stitches parallel, as shown in diagram B. It is not necessary to match stitch for stitch when shading. Add extra stitches until you cover the area, as shown in diagram C. As long as you carefully follow the colour and stitch direction charts, you will get the required effect.

PREPARATION

When thread painting, use a good quality hoop large enough to fit the entire design. If stitching on fine fabric, bind the inner ring of the hoop with bias binding or cotton tape, as shown in diagram 1. This helps to hold the fabric and prevent it slipping while stitching.

If using wool or heavy fabric I do not bind the hoop as I find the binding makes it too hard to get the hoop on and it tends to spring off.

Using a lead pencil, trace each design using white tissue paper. This paper can be purchased at any newsagent in the gift-wrap department. Outline the design as shown on the tracing pattern provided for each design. It is not necessary to trace the stitch direction lines. These can be added when stitching, as described in diagram A on page 10.

Fold your fabric in quarters to find the centre and mark with a pin. Centre the tracing on the right side of the fabric. Pin in position, making sure the tracing is not back to front, which is quite an easy mistake to make.

Carefully tack along the design lines. The tacking stitches should be approximately 9mm (3/8″) when working large areas, for example, down the rabbit's back, but when tacking a more detailed area such as his eye, nose or little paws, then you can reduce the size of your stitches to 3–5mm (1/8″–1/4″).

When tacking, I always use similar coloured sewing cotton to the project I am working on. This helps if there are any small fibres left in the embroidery after removing the tacking thread, as they will not show. Sometimes, instead of removing the tacking, I cheat and embroider over the top of the tacking threads!

Once you have tacked on the design, dampen the paper (just the tacked area) with a little water. Do not soak, just dampen the tissue paper. Then using a pair of tweezers or the end of your scissors, carefully remove the tissue paper by pushing slightly in

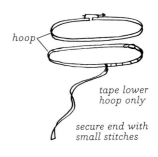

hoop

tape lower
hoop only

secure end with
small stitches

*place work over bound hoop,
secure top hoop, keep work taut*

thread painting

beehive from honey bunny

felt panels

turnips from carrot bunny

*2 felt circles
on top of
one another*

a downward motion and then away from the tacking. This motion will help remove the paper from underneath the actual stitches and helps stop it from catching. You can remove any remaining pieces of tissue using tweezers. I find overlocker tweezers are ideal for removing tacking stitches.

Some of the designs require small pieces of felt or other thick fabric to pad out a feature on the design. Following the tracing pattern, cut out the piece of felt and couch in position with matching sewing cotton.

Embroider over the felt using interlocked straight stitch, carefully following the colour and stitch direction charts.

REMEMBER THESE IMPORTANT RULES

1. Work on a hoop and keep your fabric taut.
2. Keep your tension relaxed and do not pull tightly on the thread.
3. Do not overfill an area with too many stitches.
4. As you work, pierce the fabric with single up and down stitches.

If you remember these rules you should keep your work smooth and the fabric will not buckle.

ADAPTABLE PANELS

I designed these twelve designs to be used for almost any project, a rug, a library bag, or on each corner of a bed quilt. You could include them with your quilting, embroider one on a sweatshirt, the list is endless.

The designs are suitable for both male and female projects. If you wish to make one more feminine, just add more flowers; for a more masculine look, add more greenery.

My designs have been worked on our magnificent Australian wool blanketing, but any other medium weight fabric is suitable.

I have quilted my panels into a wall hanging, combining the wool blanketing with calico damask and green patterned cotton. Each panel has been outlined with green mini piping.

BUNNIES HEADS

Work the eyes, nose and mouth as described on page 16. Pupils should be half the size of the whole eye area,.make sure the corners of the eye are not too sharp giving a mean appearance.

Work the nose and the base of the ear in the stronger pink colour, the remaining inner ear to be worked in the softer pink. Blend the two colours by interlocking the stitches with the stitches already worked

Work around the eye areas, nose and mouth as shown below. Next use colours indicated for each bunny and lock into the stitches you have already worked. Continue with the next colours indicated on your pattern, again locking into the previous colours.

BUNNIES TAILS

The rabbit's tails, only visible on some rabbits, depending on the angle at which they are standing, are embroidered in a small cluster of ghiordes knots in 1 strand of ecru, white or a combination of ecru and white.

This easy stitch is also known as single knot tufting or Turkey work. It is a group of very closely worked loops, cut and trimmed to shape. I secure each loop with a tiny straight stitch to stop the loop sliding undone. Work to a rhythm: …stitch, loop, stitch, loop, stitch. The cut loops can be combed and fluffed out to form a soft tail. If you feel the tail is not quite large enough you can always add a few more stiches, but be careful not to make the tail too large.

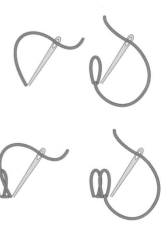

GHIORDES KNOT

thread painting

STITCHES & TECHNIQUES IN THIS BOOK...

Backstitch

Blanket stitch

Bullion knot

Cast-on stitch

Couching

Cross stitch

Detached chain

Fly stitch

French knot

Ghiordes knot

Interlocked straight stitch

Lattice couching

Palestrina stitch

Raised stem stitch

Satin stitch

Split stitch

Stem stitch

Straight stitch

NEEDLES IN THIS BOOK...

Chenille

size 22   wool embroidery

Crewel

size 9   silk and cotton embroidery and tacking

Straw

size 1   bullion knots, Ghiordes knots and French knots

the projects

bunnies in my garden

watering bunny
stitch instructions

eyes Outline the shape of each eye with Y in tiny backstitches to obtain the right shape and size. Once you have the right shape, fill in the pupil with satin stitch. Embroider the two little straight stitches to form the illusion of eyelashes after the face is completed.

DIAGRAM 1

mouth Continue with Y and keep the left side slightly shorter than the right side as shown in diagram 1.

DIAGRAM 2

nose Fill in with three tiny stitches using K, keeping the nose small as shown in diagram 2.

DIAGRAM 3

head, ears, body, paws & feet Using D, stitch around the right eye area and then around the left eye, as shown in diagram 3.
Embroider the whisker pads and a few uneven straight stitches above the nose and one stitch under the mouth. Complete the head and ears carefully following the stitch direction and colour charts. When working the paws, hips and feet, stitch the darker areas first, then the medium and the lightest colour last.
Partially outline the body and feet in A, adding straight stitches to form the shadow between the toes.
Stitch the tummy in D and E in interlocked straight stitch, emphasising E under the chin and chest.

jacket Work the collar in E using satin stitch and outline in Z. Following the colour and stitch direction charts, complete the jacket fabric. Using palestrina stitch and K, trim the jacket cuffs and edge. Next work the partial outlines on the inside of the cuffs and the lower edge of the jacket, the elbow and creases in the sleeve in Z.

hat Using R, embroider the hat in raised stem stitch following the instructions for "Barrow Bunny". To stitch the hatband, work a long stitch from one side of

watering
bunny

watering bunny
stitch instructions *[continued]*

DIAGRAM 4

the crown to the other using S, secure and couch in position as shown in diagram 4.

To form the bow, stitch two ghiordes knots for the loops and small stem stitches in a 'S' shape for the ribbons. Let one ribbon fall on the other side of the brim as shown in diagram 4.

Underline the hat brim with Z in stem stitch and then work one row of straight stitch in Q directly under Z to form the shadow under the hat.

watering can Following the stitch direction chart, stitch the first layer of the watering can in F in vertical interlocked straight stitch. This first layer helps pad the watering can and give it a three dimensional appearance. For the second layer, continue in F, working the spout in satin stitch and the drum in interlocked straight stitch. To form the handles work two rows of small stem stitch.

Outline the watering can in Z, stitching the little holes in the spout across the grain of the satin stitch to stop them from disappearing.

lamp post Embroider the post using interlocked straight stitch, carefully following the stitch direction and colour charts. Stitch the fancy ironwork in small stem stitch. Add the lamplight using satin stitch in X. Outline the lamp post in Z.

climbing rose Weave the stem of the rose around the lamp post as shown in the colour location chart in small split stitches using Q.

Add the leaves in detached chains in V and fill each centre with a straight stitch as shown in diagram 5.

The whole leaf does not have to be filled in. Remember that in real life not every leaf is at the same stage of development or size so don't worry if yours are not!

For each rose, embroider a double French knot in M and then couch the centre. Changing to K and then L, stitch small straight stitches around the knot, slightly overlapping each stitch to form the petals as shown in diagram 6.

detached chain stitch  straight stitch

DIAGRAM 5

french knot  K

L

DIAGRAM 6

tail Embroider the tail using E in a small cluster of ghiordes knots. Secure each loop with a tiny straight stitch. Work to a rhythm stitch, loop, stitch, loop, stitch. Cut the loops and comb out the threads to form a soft tail.

alyssum Work clusters of 3 wrap French knots at the base of the lamp post in N, O and P, keeping the colours in groups rather than spreading them evenly.

marigolds Embroider the leaves in I and H using fly stitch and the stem in H in straight stitch. Stitch each flower as shown in diagram 7 with 2 strands of J.

8 wrap stitches — 4 straight stitches

DIAGRAM 7

pink gerbera Stitch the stems with three split stitches in V and changing to U, add double detached chains for the leaves. Embroider the flowers with W in detached chains.

grass & earth Embroider the grass with horizontal interlocked straight stitch in H and the earth in B.

water Add water to the watering can using U and horizontal interlocked straight stitch. Embroider the water coming from the spout with tiny straight stitches and for the puddles of water, finish with three split stitches on each side of the gerbera clump.

watering bunny
tracing pattern

stitch direction

first layer

2 rows
stem stitch

second layer

watering bunny
colour location

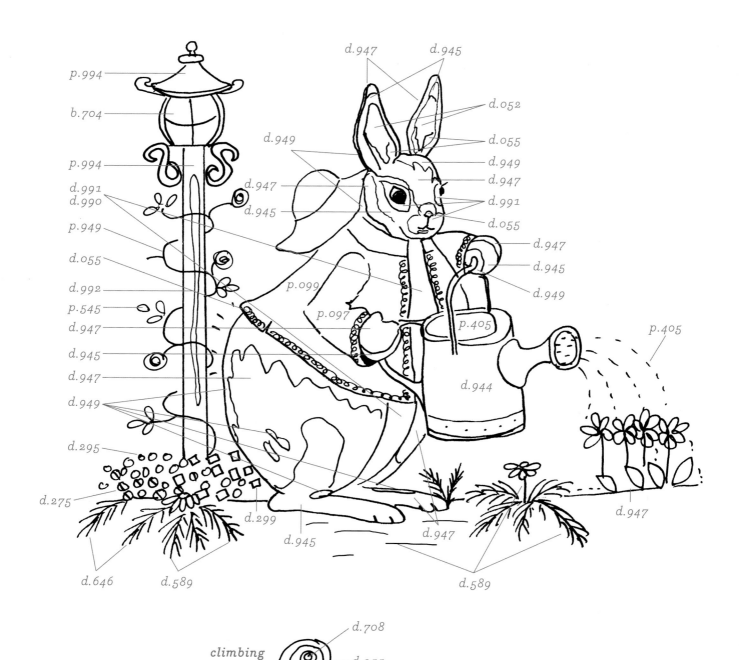

p.994

b.704

p.994

d.991
d.990

p.949

d.055

d.992

p.545

d.947

d.945

d.947

d.949

d.295

d.275

d.646

d.589

d.947

d.945

d.949

d.947

d.945

d.055

d.949

d.947

d.991

d.055

d.947

d.945

d.949

p.099

p.097

p.405

d.944

p.405

d.947

d.299

d.945

d.947

d.589

climbing roses

d.708

d.055

d.052

threads

GUMNUT YARNS 'DAISIES' 1-ply fine wool

A = d.949 ultra dk hazelnut — *head, ears, body, paws & feet*
B = d.947 dk hazelnut — *head, ears, body, paws, feet & earth*
C = d.945 med hazelnut — *head, ears, body, paws & feet*
D = d.991 ecru — *head & chest*
E = d.990 white — *collar & tail*
F = d.994 med lt pewter — *watering can, outlines & lamp*
G = d.992 vy lt pewter — *watering can & lamp post*
H = d.589 ultra dk apple green — *grass & Marigold stem*
I = d.646 med dk khaki — *Marigold leaves*
J = d.785 med apricot delight — *Marigold flower*
K = d.055 med sweet pea — *climbing rose, nose & ears*
L = d.052 vy lt sweet pea — *climbing rose & ears*
M = d.708 vy dk lemon crush — *rose centres*
N = d.275 med hyacinth — *Alyssum*
O = d.295 med lavender — *Alyssum*
P = d.299 ultra dk lavender — *Alyssum*

GUMNUT YARNS 'POPPIES' silk/wool

Q = p.949 ultra dk hazelnut — *rose stem & shadow under hat*
R = p.945 med hazelnut — *hat*
S = p.099 ultra dk raspberry — *jacket & hat ribbon*
T = p.097 dk raspberry — *jacket*
U = p. 405 med sky blue — *water*
V = p.545 med forest grove — *Gerbera leaves & rose leaves*
W = p.016 med dk watermelon — *Gerbera flowers*

GUMNUT YARNS 'BUDS' perle silk

X = b.704 med lt lemon crush — *lamplight*

D.M.C. stranded cotton

Y = 310 black — *eyes*

RAJMAHAL art silk

Z = r.25 dk grey — *outlines*

> All embroidery is worked with the fabric in a hoop. Use one strand of thread unless otherwise stated.

topiary bunny
stitch instructions

DIAGRAM 1

DIAGRAM 2

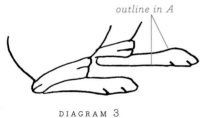

outline in A

DIAGRAM 3

eyes using tiny backstitches, outline the shape of the full eye with AA. Once you have the right shape, fill in the pupil with satin stitch as shown in diagram 1. The other eye is worked with 2 or 3 straight stitches. The eyelashes are each embroidered with a single straight stitch.

nose fill in the nose with approximately three tiny straight stitches in E, building the stitches up rather than spreading them out.

head, ears, paws & feet work these areas in interlocked straight stitch. Start stitching around the eye and then the whisker pads in D. The top of the nose has a few tiny straight stitches in C as shown in diagram 2.
Work the darker areas in A and then complete the face with B and C, interlocking the stitches. Stitch the ears, paws and feet following the stitch direction and colour charts. Partially outline the feet in small straight stitches using A. Add stitches to suggest the splits between the toes as shown in diagram 3.

shirt embroider the braces after the shirt fabric is complete. Stitch the collar and darker areas including the outline of the sleeve in R. Continue the sleeve in T and the rest of the shirt in S. Using AA, add partial outlines to the sleeve including the little creases in the sleeve. Continue working with AA and outline the collar and paws.

trousers work the darker areas in interlocked straight stitch in U noting the change in stitch direction for the trouser cuffs. Complete with V.
Work the waistband in V with two rows of stem stitch.
Partially outline the trousers in straight stitch in EE. Work the top stitching on the trousers, together with the pocket and trouser fly in tiny straight stitches.

shears embroider the handles using Z. Lay four long straight stitches the full

topiary
bunny

length of the handles, laying these stitches almost on top of each other. Secure and couch down with small even satin stitch. When couching, bring the needle from underneath the four straight stitches rather than from the side. This gives a rounder shape to the handles.

Work the blades in Y in interlocked straight stitch. Outline each blade in AA and partially outline the underside of the handles in EE.

topiary tree   stitch the crown of the tree in detached chain stitch. Work the foliage in all directions and embroider on top of some previously worked stitching. This is a good way to get a bushy effect. Follow the colour chart for colour changes. The falling leaves are worked in X in detached chain stitch. For the stem, using DD, lay six straight lines from the tree foliage to the top centre of the plant pot. Keep these lines close together and couch in place with 1 strand of DD. Next, using BB, work one row of stem stitch close to the right side of the stem. Using EE, work the stake in stem stitch and place 3 horizontal straight stitches across the stem to form stake ties.

plant pot   stitch the plant pot using the stitch direction chart as a guide and as shown in diagram on page 31.

grass   using horizontal straight and split stitch, work in O, P and Q. Don't allow your stitches to become too long. Use O to the right of the pot to form a

shadow.

alyssum stitch three to four wrap French knots in L and M to form the Alyssum flowers. Couch each knot with a small stitch.

forget-me-nots using N, stitch the flowers using the same method as for the alyssum flowers.

hollyhock flowers & leaves embroider as shown in diagrams 5, 6 and 7 below, following the colour chart. Start with the stem and buds, then the leaves and flowers.

braces work the braces in Za in chain stitch. Work two detached chains over the waistband for button tabs. The buttons are double wrap French knots stitched with L. Couch to secure.

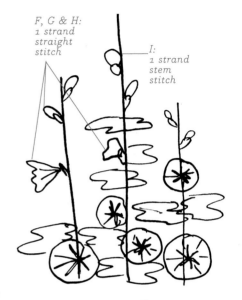

DIAGRAM 5

DIAGRAM 6

flowers
1 strand straight stitch

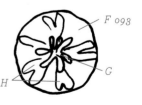

DIAGRAM 7

topiary bunny
tracing pattern

stitch direction

topiary bunny
colour location

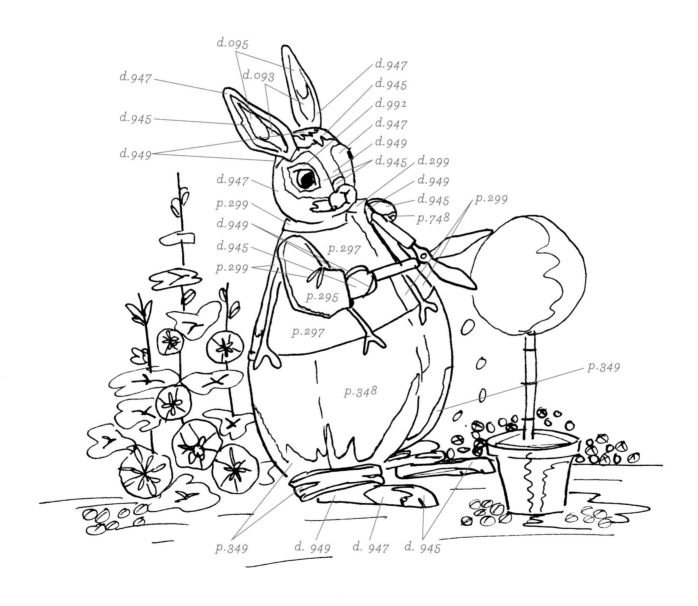

d.095

d.093

d.947

d.947

d.945

d.949

d.947

p.299

d.949

d.945

p.299

d.947

d.945

d.991

d.947

d.949

d.945   d.299

d.949

d.945

p.748

p.299

p.297

p.295

p.297

p.348

p.349

p.349   d. 949   d. 947   d. 945

threads

GUMNUT YARNS 'DAISIES' 1-ply fine wool

A = d.949 ultra dk hazelnut	*head, ears, paws & feet*
B = d.947 dk hazelnut	*head, ears & feet*
C = d.945 med hazelnut	*head, ears, paws & feet*
D = d.991 ecru	*head*
E = d.095 med raspberry	*ears & nose*
F = d.093 lt raspberry	*ears & Hollyhock flowers*
G = d.058 vy dk sweet pea	*Hollyhock flowers*
H = d.055 med sweet pea	*Hollyhock flowers*
I = d.648 vy dk khaki	*Hollyhock leaves*
J = d.646 med dk khaki	*Hollyhock leaves*
K = d.643 lt khaki	*Hollyhock leaves*
L = d.708 vy dk lemon crush	*Alyssum flowers*
M = d.785 med apricot delight	*Alyssum flowers*
N = d.386 med dk cornflower	*Forget-me-not flowers*
O = d.549 ultra dk forest grove	*grass*
P = d.547 dk forest grove	*grass*
Q = d.545 med forest grove	*grass*

GUMNUT YARNS 'POPPIES' silk/wool

R = p.299 ultra dk lavender	*shirt*
S = p.297 dk lavender	*shirt*
T = p.295 med lavender	*shirt*
U = p.349 ultra dk denim	*trousers*
V = p.348 vy dk denim	*trousers*
W = p.589 ultra dk apple green	*topiary leaves*
X = p.587 dark apple green	*topiary leaves*
Y = p.994 med lt pewter	*shear blades*
Z = p.748 very dk daffodil	*shear handles*
Za = p.857 dk salmon pink	*braces*

D.M.C. stranded cotton

AA = 310 black	*eyes, mouth & outlining*

D.M.C. BRODER MÉDICIS 1-ply wool

BB = 8300 dk brown	*pot, topiary stem*
CC = 8320 med brown	*pot, topiary stem*
DD = 8302 tan	*pot, topiary stem*
EE = black	*outlines on pot, topiary stake & ties*

All embroidery is worked with the fabric in a hoop. Use one strand of thread unless otherwise stated.

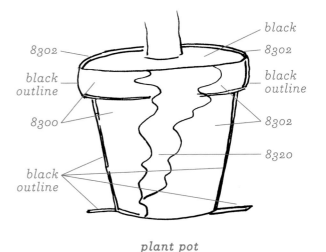

black
8302

black
8302

black
outline

black
outline

8302

8300

8320

black
outline

plant pot

potting bunny
stitch instructions

eyes outline the shape of the full eye using DD in tiny backstitches. Embroider the pupil in satin stitch and the eye on the left side with two or three small straight stitches. Work the little eyelashes after the face is complete.

mouth work the mouth and underside of the nose with DD in small straight stitches.

head, ears, paws & feet using D, stitch around the eye area following the stitch direction chart. Then work the whisker pads in D. Change to C and stitch around the eye area, locking these stitches into those embroidered in D. Work the darker areas in A and the remaining area in B. Complete the ears, paws and feet referring to the colour and stitch direction charts.

nose embroider two to three tiny straight stitches with E, keeping the nose small by building the stitches up rather than laying them out.

eyelashes using DD, embroider a single straight stitch for each eyelash.

jacket collar work the collar in satin stitch using G. For the back of the sailor collar, satin stitch would be too long so it is better to use two or three split stitches.

trousers continuing with G, stitch the darker areas first then change to H to complete the trousers.

potting
bunny

potting bunny
stitch instructions [continued]

jacket using R, work the darker areas first and then change to S to finish the jacket fabric. Take note of the stitch direction changes on the main sleeve. Work the piping in G using split stitch. Change to straight stitch for the jacket lining at the cuffs. Embroider the buttons on the front of the jacket in H using double wrap French knots and couch with a single stitch to secure.

Using G, stitch the jacket back tab in straight stitch and then work a double French knot and couch to secure.

table using V, W and X, embroider the table following the stitch direction and colour charts.

azalea pot (on the potting table)...work the pot in BB and CC and outline in DD with straight stitch.

Embroider the azalea leaves, working one straight stitch in U for the stem adding the leaves in detached chains.

Using Y and working from the centre, stitch the azalea flowers with eight detached chains and place a double French knot in the centre. Couch down the knot with a single stitch.

plant pots embroider in interlocked straight stitch using A and B. Keep the merging of the two colours uneven as this gives the pots a more natural and aged appearance as shown in diagram 1.

Partially outline each of the pots in Q using small straight stitches.

watsonia embroider the leaves with M in interlocked straight stitch. As you work, pierce the stitches as shown in diagram 2.

Stitch the flowers using J in detached chains worked in a downward direction.

*dummy caption
unnatural appearance*

*dummy caption
natural appearance*

DIAGRAM 1

DIAGRAM 2

daisy work the stems in L and using K, embroider each of the flowers with four to five detached chains. Add a double wrap French knot in D for the centre and couch in position.

hydrangea embroider the leaves in fly stitch using I, L and M. Keep the leaves close together and place in different directions to give the plant a bushy appearance. Add two fallen leaves at the base of the pot. For the flowers, stitch circular clumps of double wrap French knots in N, O and P. Couch each knot to secure in place.

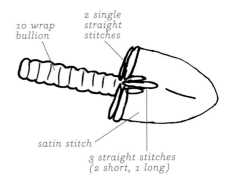

10 wrap bullion

2 single straight stitches

satin stitch

3 straight stitches (2 short, 1 long)

DIAGRAM 3

spade work the handle in a ten wrap bullion knot in T and couch in position. Embroider two straight stitches each side of the handle and three small straight stitches in the centre as shown in diagram 3.
Complete the spade with W in satin stitch.

potting soil stitch the soil falling from the spade, on the potting table and from the knocked over daisy, in single, double and triple French knots using A.

potting bunny
tracing pattern

stitch direction

potting bunny
colour location

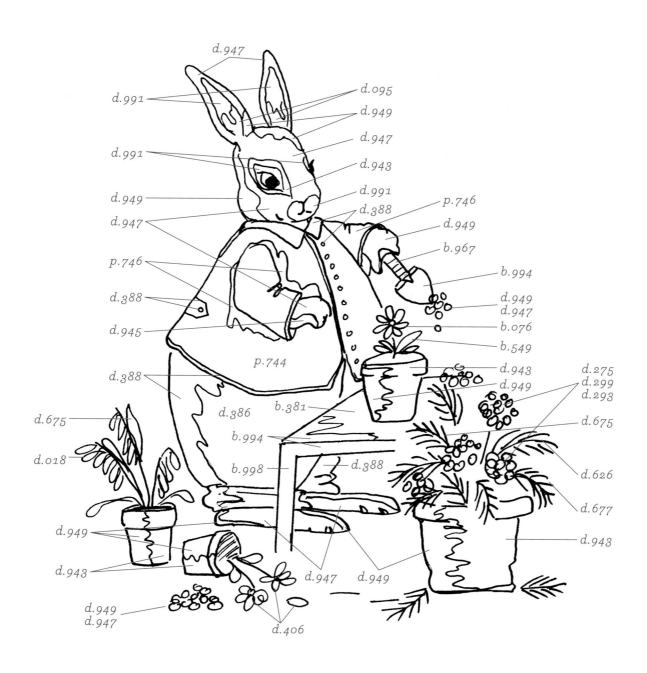

threads

GUMNUT YARNS 'DAISIES' 1-ply xx

A = d. 949 ultra dk hazelnut	*head, ears, paws, feet & plant pots*
B = d.947 dk hazelnut	*head, ears, paws, feet & plant pots*
C = d.943 lt hazelnut	*head & paws*
D = d.991ecru	*face & daisy centres*
E = d.095med raspberry	*ears*
F = d.093lt raspberry	*ears*
G = d.388vy dk cornflower	*trousers, collar, buttons & jacket piping*
H = d.386 med dk cornflower	*trousers & buttons*
I = d.675 med olive	*Watsonia leaves & hydrangea leaves*
J = d.018 vy dk watermelon	*Watsonia flowers*
K = d.406 med dk sky blue	*Daisy flower*
L = d.626 med dk eucalypt	*Hydrangea leaves & Daisy stem*
M = d.677 dk olive	*Hydrangea leaves*
N = d.275 med hyacinth	*Hydrangea flowers*
O = d.299 ultra dk lavender	*Hydrangea flowers*
P = d.293 lt lavender	*Hydrangea flowers*
Q = d.998 vy dk pewter	*outlines*

> All embroidery is worked with the fabric in a hoop. Use one strand of thread unless otherwise stated.

GUMNUT YARNS 'POPPIES' silk/wool

R = p.746 med dk daffodil	*jacket*
S = p.744 med lt daffodil	*jacket*

GUMNUT YARNS 'BUDS' perle silk

T = b.967 dark chocolate dip	*spade handle*
U = b.549 ultra dk forest grove	*azalea leaves*
V = b.998 vy dk pewter	*table leg & outlines*
W = b.994 med lt pewter	*table & spade*
X = b.381ultra lt cornflower	*table*
Y = b.076 med dk carnation	*Azalea flowers*

D.M.C. BRODER MÉDICIS 1-ply wool

AA = 8320 tan	*Azalea pot*
BB = 8306 dk brown	*Azalea pot*
CC = black	*Azalea pot outline*

D.M.C. stranded cotton

DD = 310 black	*eyes & mouth*

letter bunny
stitch instructions

eye outline the shape of the eye with DD in tiny backstitch to obtain the right size and shape and fill in the pupil with satin stitch.

mouth as this rabbit stands sideways, only half of his mouth is visible. Embroider with three tiny straight stitches in FF.

nose work two or three tiny straight stitches in G, building the stitches up to keep the nose small.

head, ears, paws & feet embroider around the eye area in E and then stitch the whisker pads. Next work the darker areas in C, keeping these areas to a minimum to prevent the face from becoming too dark. Complete the head and ears following the stitch direction and colour charts. If, after you have completed the rabbit's head, it looks too dark you can soften the colour by working a few extra stitches of A into C. It is wonderful how just one or two stitches can change the look of embroidery without the odious task of unpicking. Complete the paws and feet, partially outlining the feet and adding a shadow between the toes.

jacket using J, stitch the collar by working two layers of satin stitch. Outline with I in split stitch. Continuing with I, outline the right sleeve in split stitch and then work the darker areas of the jacket in interlocked straight stitch. Change to J and complete the jacket, outlining the far left sleeve in split stitch. Add three buttons, stitching with EE in double wrap French knots couched in place.

trousers carefully following the colour and stitch direction guides, stitch the darker areas in K and complete with L. Partially outline the trousers and cuffs with K and then at the top of the cuff with DD.

letter
bunny

letter bunny
stitch instructions [continued]

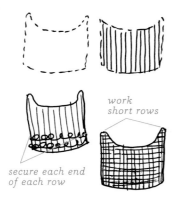

work short rows

secure each end of each row

stem stitch

DIAGRAM 1

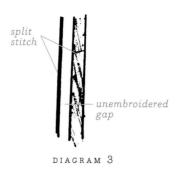

DIAGRAM 2

split stitch

unembroidered gap

DIAGRAM 3

tail embroider the tail using F in a small cluster of ghiordes knots. Add a few stitches in E at the top of the tail. Secure each loop with a tiny straight stitch. Work to a rhythm …stitch, loop, stitch, loop, stitch. Cut the loops and comb out the threads to form a soft tail.

letter using F, outline a square shape and fill in with satin stitch and outline to form an envelope in FF.

mail bag using CC, embroider in raised stem stitch following the instructions for the hat in "Barrow Bunny". Work vertical uprights and then alternate rows of BB and CC. To shape the top of the bag, simply work separate short rows as shown in diagram 1.

Add the top edge of the bag in stem stitch as shown in diagram 1.

To stitch the handle, using 2 strands of CC, make one long plumb-line from the shoulder to the bag top edge and a shorter line from the forearm to the bag. Changing to 1 strand, couch to secure. Stitch from the top of the bag over the shoulder and then from under the forearm to the top of the opposite side of the bag as shown in diagram 2.

Using C, shade inside the mailbag in interlocked straight stitch and outline in stem stitch.

letter box using U, stitch the pole in vertical rows of split stitch, starting with the wider part of the pole and, leaving a gap, then a single row of split stitch as shown in diagram 3.

Following the stitch direction and colour charts, stitch the letter box in satin stitch. Partially outline in DD. Embroider the number and slit in DD and outline in EE.

climbing rose weave the stem around the letterbox pole in S using stem stitch. Add the leaves in detached chains with R. Stitch the roses in clusters of triple wrap French knots in Q, couching each knot with a small stitch to secure.

alyssum using O and P, work double and triple French knots. Stitch in small clusters of the same colour rather that spread the two colours evenly as this looks more natural. Couch each knot as you work to keep them secure.

forget-me-nots work triple French knots in N and couch in place.

grass embroider in Z and AA in horizontal straight and split stitches.

freesias stitch the flowers in large detached chains in M and Y, placing them in different directions. Add the stems in straight stitch with AA and Z.

large leaves place next to the letter box pole, working in fly stitch and using R.

robin red breast following the enlarged stitch direction and colour charts, embroider in satin stitch.

letter bunny
tracing pattern

stitch direction

letter bunny
colour location

d.994

d.095

d.093

d.998

d.994

d.992

d.991

d.095

d.867

d.865

d.865

d.867

d.990

d.626

d.628

d.708 b.785

d.990

d.807

d.992

d.677

d.947

d.969

5282

310

d.018

d.969

d.545

d.949

d.708 b.785

d.679

b.275
b.273

d.406

d.677 d.992

d.994 d.628

single wrap french knot
310

s.865

s.867

s.865

s.859

straight stitch 310

threads

GUMNUT YARNS 'DAISIES' 1-ply fine wool

A = d.994 med lt pewter	*head, paws & feet*
B = d.992 vy lt pewter	*head, paws & feet*
C = d.998 vy dk pewter	*feet outline & head*
D = d.947 dark hazelnut	*letter box*
E = d.991 ecru	*face & tail*
F = d.990 white	*letter & tail*
G = d.095 med raspberry	*nose & ears*
H = d.093 lt raspberry	*ears*
I = d.867 dk flesh	*jacket*
J = d.865 med flesh	*jacket*
K = d.628 vy dk eucalypt	*trousers*
L = d.626 med dk eucalypt	*trousers*
M = d.708 vy dk lemon crush	*Freesias*
N = d.406 med dk sky blue	*Forget-me-not*
O = d.275 med hyacinth	*Alyssum*
P = d.273 lt hyacinth	*Alyssum*
Q = d.018 vy dk watermelon	*roses*
R = d.677 dk olive	*leaves*
S = d.549 ultra dk forest grove	*grass & rose stem*
T = d.545 med forest grove	*rose leaves*
U = d.969 ultra dk chocolate dip	*letter box*

GUMNUT YARNS 'STARS' stranded silk

V = s.867 dk flesh	*Robin*
W = s.865 med flesh	*Robin*
X = s.859 ultra dk salmon pink	*Robin*

GUMNUT YARNS 'BUDS' perle silk

Y = b.785 med apricot delight	*Freesias*
Z = b.677 dk olive	*grass*
AA = b.679 ultra dk olive	*grass*
BB = b.969 ultra dk chocolate dip	*mail bag*
CC = b.966 med dk chocolate dip	*mail bag*

D.M.C. stranded cotton

DD = 310 black	*outlines*

D.M.C. stranded metallic thread

EE = 5282 gold	*buttons & letter box*

RAJMAHAL art silk

FF = r.25 dk grey	*outlines*

> All embroidery is worked with the fabric in a hoop. Use one strand of thread unless otherwise stated.

letter bunny

mowing bunny
stitch instructions

eyes outline the shape of the right eye with AA in tiny backstitches and when you have the correct size and shape fill in the pupil with satin stitch. To form the left eye, work two small straight stitches close together. Stitch the eyelashes later.

mouth continuing with AA, work the mouth in straight stitch.

nose using F, fill in the nose with three tiny straight stitches. Build up the stitches so the nose remains small and a little raised.

DIAGRAM 1

head, ears, eyelashes, paws & feet starting with the eye areas, work around the right eye in D and then stitch two straight stitches around the left eye as shown in diagram 1.

Following diagram 2, work a straight stitch on each eye to form the illusion of eyelashes.

Now work the darkest areas of the head in A, keeping these areas small. Do not allow the stitches to become too long as it will make the rabbit look too dark and the project will loose its gentle appearance.

Continue stitching the rest of the face, ears, paws and feet following the stitch direction and colour charts. Partially outline the feet and between the toes in AA as shown in diagram 3.

DIAGRAM 2

collar & cuffs embroider in U in satin stitch.

DIAGRAM 3

jacket outline the sleeves in J and then complete the jacket using J and K. Once the jacket is complete, partially outline in J.

mowing bunny

mowing bunny
stitch instructions [continued]

DIAGRAM 4

DIAGRAM 5

DIAGRAM 6

DIAGRAM 7

DIAGRAM 8

DIAGRAM 9

trousers stitch the darker areas first with H and then complete in I.

mower the wheels are worked in two layers. For the first layer, using Z, fill in as shown in diagram 4 below with interlocked straight stitch, keeping the edge of your work neat. Now work a row of small stem stitch for the thinner side.

For the second layer, continuing with Z, couch a row of satin stitch over the top of the first layer as shown in diagram 5 below.

For the right wheel centre, using A and then B, work alternate straight stitches from the centre outwards as shown in diagram 6 below.

For the mower blades, work alternate rows of straight stitches using AA, BB and V, then a row of zigzag on the far side of the mower as shown in diagram 7 below.

To embroider the mower handle, using W, stitch a guide line or plumb-line from one paw to the other as shown in diagram 8 below.

Next stitch another two plumb-lines from the centre of the right wheel to the top of the left (far side) wheel as shown in diagram 9 below.

Now make a plumb-line from the centre of the first line and to the top of the second two as shown in diagram 10 below.

Work three more long stitches over the top of these stitches. It is important that these stitches are straight but not tight. Keep these stitches almost on top of each other. Carefully couch over the top of the long stitches bringing your needle up from underneath the stitches rather than from the side. When you take your needle back through the fabric, pierce the fabric under the strands rather than to the side so as to give the handle a round tubular effect. Keep your couching stitches as even as possible. See diagram 11 below.

Add the bolts holding the handle to the mower with three straight stitches in Z.

foxgloves embroider the stems with Q in backstitch and the small single leaves with R in detached chain stitch.

For the pink flowers, work in L and stitch detached chains up the stem of the flower, reducing the size of the chains as you work higher up the flower stem. Fill in the centre of each flower with a small straight stitch in G.

Stitch the blue flowers in the same manner as the pink, using N for the detached chains and complete the centres with M.

DIAGRAM 10

alyssum embroider these tiny flowers in O and P with French knots in both double and triple wraps. Couch down to secure.

large leaf work in Q in fly stitch.

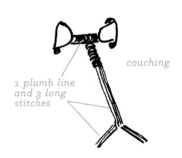

couching

1 plumb line and 3 long stitches

DIAGRAM 11

grass stitch the mown lawn in a mix of R, X and Y in interlocked straight stitch. Work the unmown lawn in vertical straight stitches in X and Y. Embroider some stitches at an angle to give the grass an untidy, natural look. Add the cuttings in X, using small straight stitches.

birds using M, stitch long 'M' shapes in straight stitch as shown in diagram 12.

add extra stitches to form thicker part of the wing

DIAGRAM 12

lavender embroider the stems in straight stitch using S. Work the flowers in eight wrap bullion knots with T. Couch down in the centre of the wraps. Complete with two tiny straight stitches on the top in a 'V' shape.

tail stitch the tail using D in a small cluster of ghiordes knots. Secure each loop with a tiny straight stitch. Work to a rhythm …stitch, loop, stitch, loop, stitch. Cut the loops and comb out the threads to form a soft tail.

mowing bunny

mowing bunny
tracing pattern

stitch direction

couching lines

mowing bunny
colour location

d.018

d.994   d.095

d.093

d.994

d.998

d.991

d.299   d.992

d.297

d.299

d.991

d.018
d.058

d.406
d.408

d.297

d.299

s.293

d.992

d.297

b.994

d.235

d.055

d.052

d.549   d.785   d.708

d.992   d.994   d.055

310
d.998
d.994

p.867

p.679
p.677

d.677

310
s.998

threads

GUMNUT YARNS 'DAISIES' 1-ply fine wool

A= d.998 vy dk pewter	*head, ears, feet & mower*
B = d.994 med lt pewter	*head, ears, feet & mower*
C = d.992 vy lt pewter	*head, ears, paws & feet*
D = d.991 ecru	*head, paws, feet & tail*
E = d.095 med raspberry	*ears & nose*
F = d.093 lt raspberry	*ears*
G = d.058 vy dk sweet pea	*Foxglove flowers*
H = d.055 med sweet pea	*trousers*
I = d.052 vy lt sweet pea	*trousers*
J = d.299 ultra dk lavender	*jacket*
K = d.297 dk lavender	*jacket*
L = d.018 vy dk watermelon	*Foxglove flowers*
M = d.408 vy dk sky blue	*Foxglove flowers & birds*
N = d.406 med dk sky blue	*Foxglove flowers*
O = d.708 vy dk lemon crush	*Alyssum*
P = d.785 med apricot delight	*Alyssum*
Q = d.549 ultra dk forest grove	*flower stems & large leaf*
R = d.547 dk forest grove	*small leaves & mown lawn*
S = d.677 dk olive	*lavender stems*
T= d.235 med pansy	*lavender*

GUMNUT YARNS 'STARS' stranded silk

U = s.293 lt lavender	*jacket collar & cuffs*
V = s.998 vy dk pewter	*mower blades*

GUMNUT YARNS 'BUDS' perle silk

W = b.994 med lt pewter	*lawn mower handle*

GUMNUT YARNS 'POPPIES' silk/wool

X = p.679 ultra dk olive	*mown lawn & uncut grass*
Y = p.677 dk olive	*mown lawn & uncut grass*
Z = p.867 dk flesh	*mower wheels*

D.M.C. stranded cotton

AA = 310 black	*eyes, mouth & mower blades*

D.M.C. stranded metallic thread

BB = 5283 silver	*mower blades*

honey bunny
stitch instructions

eye outline the eye in W to obtain the right shape and fill in the pupil with satin stitch.

DIAGRAM 1

mouth continuing with W, embroider the mouth with small straight stitches, including a very small part of the rabbit's right side as shown in diagram 1.

nose embroider two or three tiny straight stitches in E and build up the nose.

head, paws & feet embroider the ears after the beekeeper's hat is completed. Start the head by working in D, stitching around the eye and then the whisker pads and chin. Work in interlocked straight stitch. Change to C and stitch from the left whisker pad and around the area just worked around the eye, interlocking the stitches. Complete the head following the stitch direction and colour charts. Embroider the paws and feet, partially outlining the feet and between the toes.

tacked outline

hat using the tacked outline in diagram 2 below as a guide, stitch the brim of the hat and then the crown. Embroider with U and work the upright stitches as shown in diagram 2. Secure each end of the thread by stitching a tiny straight stitch and then stitching back into itself.

Stitch the crown flat to keep the ears and hat in proportion.

Now work raised stem stitch from left to right. Before you start each row secure the thread to the left of the first upright stitch and when you get to the end of the row secure the thread on the right hand side of the last thread. Cut the thread and return to the left hand side and start the second row remembering to secure the thread first. This process of securing the thread keeps the hat in the correct shape. Using G, stitch the hatband using stem stitch and the shadow under the brim in straight stitch.

secure stitches

DIAGRAM 2

honey
bunny

stitch instructions [*continued*]

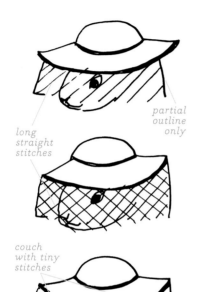

long straight stitches

partial outline only

couch with tiny stitches

DIAGRAM 3

beekeeper's net embroider in Z using lattice couching as shown in diagram 3. If this looks slightly uneven, don't be concerned, as the effect is more natural.

ears using interlocked straight stitch, embroider the ears, carefully following the stitch direction and colour charts.

jacket partially outline in G, leaving the pocket and back tab until after the fabric has been worked. Stitch the darker areas of the jacket fabric in H and complete in I. Now work the pocket and back tab in little straight stitches in G.

trousers embroider the darker areas in J and complete in K, noting the change in direction for the cuffs.

tail embroider the tail using D in a small cluster of ghiordes knots. Secure each loop with a tiny straight stitch. Work to a rhythm …stitch, loop, stitch, loop, stitch.
Cut the loops and comb out the threads to form a soft tail.

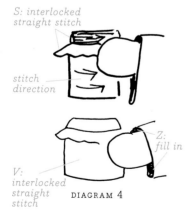

S: interlocked straight stitch

stitch direction

Z: fill in

V: interlocked straight stitch

DIAGRAM 4

honey pot stitch as shown in diagram 4. Using Z, outline the jar, lid, paw and cuff in straight stitch. Work the label using tiny backstitches. To embroider the string, cut two small pieces of T and bring both ends to the top of the jar lid as shown in diagram 5.
Tie in a double knot. Couch down the length of T at the top of the jar with a couple of tiny stitches in beige sewing cotton.

HONEY

DIAGRAM 5

beehive following the tracing pattern, cut out six pieces of cream felt and couch in position with matching sewing cotton. Embroider over the felt using interlocked straight stitch, carefully following the colour and stitch direction charts.

foliage & flowers Stitch the leaves and grass in P and Q using straight stitch, split stitch and detached chain. Add the flowers in triple wrap French knots in R, couching with a small stitch to secure.

bumble bees for each of the twelve bees, work a seven wrap bullion knot in X. Leaving a small gap, work a second seven wrap bullion knot in X. Changing to W, work a nine wrap bullion knot in the middle of the yellow bullions. Continuing with W, work a four wrap bullion knot at each end as shown in diagram 6.

To embroider the wings, using Y, work two ghiordes knots with even loops at each side of the bee as shown in diagram 7.

Secure the knots but do not cut the loops.

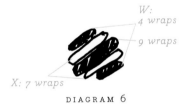

W:
4 wraps
9 wraps
X: 7 wraps

DIAGRAM 6

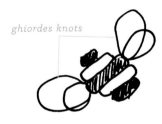

ghiordes knots

DIAGRAM 7

honey bunny

tracing pattern

*cut out in cream
coloured felt*

stitch direction

honey bunny

colour location

d.947
d.945
d.093
d.095

d.991
d.945
d.095
d.945
d.947

d.947
d.349
d.346
d.348
d.991

d.295

d.748

d.297

d.748   d.746   d.349   d.999   d.744   d.947   d.949   d.945

threads

All embroidery is worked with the fabric in a hoop. Use one strand of thread unless otherwise stated.

GUMNUT YARNS 'DAISIES' 1-ply fine wool

A = d.949 ultra dk hazelnut — *feet*
B = d.947 dk hazelnut — *head, ears, paws & feet*
C = d.945 med hazelnut — *head, ears, paws & feet*
D = d.991 ecru — *head & tail*
E = d.095 med raspberry — *ears & nose*
F = d.093 lt raspberry — *ears*
G = d.349 ultra dk denim — *jacket outline, hatband & hive*
H = d.348 vy dk denim — *jacket*
I = d.346 med dk denim — *jacket*
J = d.297 dk lavender — *trousers*
K = d.295 med lavender — *trousers*
L = d.748 vy dk daffodil — *beehive*
M = d.746 med dk daffodil — *beehive*
N = d.744 med lt daffodil — *beehive*
O = d.999 nearly black — *beehive doorway*
P = d.648 vy dk khaki — *leaves & grass*
Q = d.677 dk olive — *leaves & grass*
R = d.018 vy dk watermelon — *flowers*
S = d.058 vy dk sweet pea — *jam jar lid*

GUMNUT YARNS 'BUDS' perle silk

T = b.991 ecru — *string on jam jar*

GUMNUT YARNS 'OPALS' silk/wool

U = mid amethyst — *hat*

GUMNUT YARNS 'STARS' stranded silk

V = s.708 vy dk lemon crush — *honey jar*

D.M.C. stranded cotton

W = 310 black — *eye, mouth & bees*
X = 728 yellow — *bees*

D.M.C. stranded metallic thread

Y = 5282 gold — *bees wings*

RAJMAHAL art silk

Z = r.25 dk grey — *bee keeper's net*

chicken bunny
stitch instructions

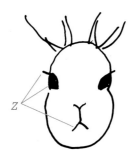

DIAGRAM 1

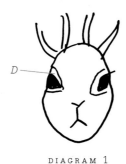

DIAGRAM 2

eyes work the outline of each eye with Z in tiny straight stitches. Fill in with satin stitch. Using D and tiny split stitches, embroider around each eye as shown in diagram 1.

mouth embroider in straight stitches with Z as shown in diagram 2.

nose fill in the nose with 2 or 3 tiny straight stitches in E, building the stitches up rather than allowing the nose to get too big. Embroider a small triangular area on top of the nose with F.

head, body, arms & feet work the whisker pads in D, being careful to follow the stitch direction chart. Complete the face following the colour chart. Work the ears, starting with the darkest areas and work towards the tip. Complete with B.
Outline the right arm in A and then stitch the rest of the body, arms and feet following the stitch direction and colour charts. Outline the feet and between the toes in O using straight stitch.

overalls complete the overalls before stitching the basket. Fill in the overalls with L first and then complete the fabric of the overalls with M. Partially outline the edge of the overalls using K and outline the side seam and chest pocket. Add the fly and stitching on the cuffs.

tail embroider the tail using D in a small cluster of ghiordes knots. Secure each loop with a tiny straight stitch. Work to a rhythm …stitch, loop, stitch, loop, stitch. Cut the loops and comb out the threads to form a soft tail.

chicken
bunny

chicken bunny
stitch instructions [continued]

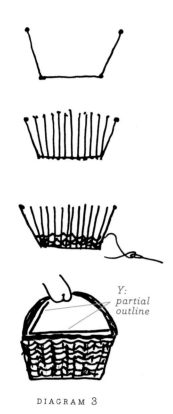

DIAGRAM 3

basket using N, stitch the shape of the basket with three long straight stitches as shown in diagram 3 .

Secure after each stitch by simply working a tiny straight stitch and then stitch back into itself. Following diagram 3, work vertical straight stitches and secure at the end of each. Embroider rows of raised stem stitch starting at the base of the basket on the left hand side and work to the right. Secure and cut the thread at the end of each row. Return to the left and secure the thread to the left of the first upright. Ease each row downward gently with your needle as you work. Embroider the handle of the basket in N. Stitch two rows of split stitch close together. Partially outline the handle and top of the basket in Z as shown in diagram 3.

chicken coop outline the timber with AA and fill in with interlocked straight stitch with P and Q. Embroider the chicken wire after the straw.

grass & flowers stitch the grass and foliage on the side of the chicken coop with I and J in straight stitch and broken chain stitch. Work the chain stitches at different angles to create a natural, slightly unkempt appearance. Embroider the flowers in three and four wrap French knots in G and H.

straw embroider the straw on the floor inside the chicken coop in T. To achieve the look of freshly laid straw, work the straight stitches in all directions and on top of each other.

chicken wire   work in AA, stitching diagonal long stitches across the coop, first one way and then the other. Couch down every point where the stitches cross as shown in diagram 4.

Don't be concerned if the wire does not look even. The coop is supposed to have been built by a rabbit so some irregularity adds character.

egg sign   embroider the outline in O in tiny straight stitch and the wording in AA.

chickens & rooster   embroider following the enlarged diagrams below.

chicken feed   stitch in AA, using tiny straight stitches coming from the rabbit's hand to the ground and around the chickens.

couch stitch

DIAGRAM 4

V: interlocked straight stitch

W: interlocked straight stitch

P: interlocked straight stitch

U: double detached chain stitch

Z: french knots

O: interlocked straight stitch

S: 2 strands straight stitch

Y: interlocked straight stitch

V: interlocked straight stitch

U: satin stitch

flecks (work last)
V: straight stitch

O: interlocked straight stitch

T: straight stitch

U: satin stitch

W: interlocked straight stitch

outline Z: straight stitch

S

T: straight stitch

Z: french knot

S: straight stitch
AA: partial outline

chicken bunny
tracing pattern

stitch direction

chicken bunny
colour location

threads

GUMNUT YARNS 'DAISIES' 1-ply fine wool

A = d.949 ultra dk hazelnut   *head, ears, body & feet*
B = d.947 dk hazelnut   *head, ears, body & feet*
C = d.945 med hazelnut   *head, ears, body & feet*
D = d.991 ecru   *head & tail*
E = d.095 med raspberry   *nose & ears*
F = d.093 lt raspberry   *ears & bridge of nose*
G = d.277 dk hyacinth   *flowers*
H = d.275 med hyacinth   *flowers*
I = d.547 dk forest grove   *leaves*
J = d.545 med forest grove   *leaves*

> All embroidery is worked
> with the fabric in a hoop.
> Use one strand of thread
> unless otherwise stated.

GUMNUT YARNS 'POPPIES' silk/wool

K = p.648 vy dk khaki   *overall outlines & stitching*
L = p. 679 ultra dk olive   *overalls*
M = p.677 dk olive   *overalls*
N = p.077 dk carnation   *basket*

GUMNUT YARNS 'STARS' stranded silk

O = s.869 ultra dk flesh   *chickens & sign post*
P = s.865 med flesh   *chickens*
Q = s.949 ultra dk hazelnut   *chickens & coop*
R = s.945 med hazelnut   *chickens & coop*
S = s.785 med apricot delight   *chicken's feet*
T = s.708 very dk lemon crush   *chicken's beak & straw*
U = s.859 ultra dk salmon pink   *chicken's and rooster's combs*
V = s.990 white   *rooster*
W = s.468 vy dk sea spray   *rooster's wing & tail feathers*
X = s.389 ultra dk cornflower   *rooster*
Y = s.349 ultra dk denim   *rooster*

D.M.C. stranded cotton

Z = 310 black   *rabbit's eyes & mouth*

RAJMAHAL art silk

AA = r.25 dk grey   *wire, outlines & seed*

carrot bunny
stitch instructions

DIAGRAM 1

eyes outline the shape of the full eye with DD in tiny backstitches to obtain the right shape. Once you have the right shape, fill in with satin stitch. Work the other eye with two small vertical straight stitches. To form the illusion of eyelashes work one straight stitch on each eye as shown in diagram 1.

mouth embroider the mouth and underside of the nose with straight stitches using DD.

nose fill in with three tiny straight stiches in E, building the stitches up rather than spreading them out.

head, ears, paws & feet using D, stitch around the eye area then work the whisker pads carefully following the stitch direction and colour charts. Next work the darker areas in A around the side of the head and the base and tip of the ears. Change to B and fill the centre of the face and right cheek area. Stitch the rest of the face with C, embroidering into the stitches already worked. Complete the ears in interlocked straight stitch following the direction and colour charts. Stitch the paws with B and C and the feet in B and partially outline in A.

jacket embroider the collar with G in satin stitch. Work the spade over the top of the rabbit's clothing to give a more three-dimensional look. Partially outline the sleeves and the hem of the jacket with L in straight stitch. Next work the darker areas in H. Complete in I, following the stitch direction chart. Stitch the buttons with three wrap French knots in L and couch to secure with a single stitch.

carrot
bunny

carrot bunny
stitch instructions [continued]

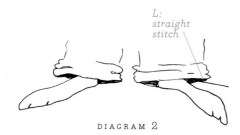

L:
straight
stitch

DIAGRAM 2

plumb
lines

all 5
plumb
lines

DIAGRAM 3a   DIAGRAM 3b

DIAGRAM 3c

trousers work the trousers in interlocked straight stitch in J. Partially outline the trousers and trouser cuffs in L. Then work the pocket stitching, being careful not to pull the stitches too tight. Remember to shade inside the trouser cuffs as shown in diagram 2.

spade using W, work a triangular plumb-line for the handle between the paws and the top of the spade shaft. Then place one long plum-line stitch from the handle to the top of the blade. Stitch a horizontal plum-line for the top of the blade. Have these stitches straight but not tight as shown in diagram 3a below. Next work four more long straight stitches on top of the plumb-line guide stitches. Keep them close together as shown in diagram 3b.
Secure the threads. Carefully couch over the top of the five plumb-line stitches keeping the couching as even as possible. When couching bring the needle up from slightly underneath the plumb-lines rather than to the side, and when taking the needle down tuck it under the guide stitches as shown in diagram 3c.
Work the blade in K and completely outline in split stitch using L.

carrots using M, starting at the top of the carrot, form a seventeen wrap bullion knot. Place the next bullion below the first and decrease the number of wraps. Continue down the carrot, decreasing the number of wraps at the end of the carrot to form a point. Some of the carrots are sticking up from the earth and therefore do not need to be full length. Stitch one straight stitch between each bullion in AA. Do not try to keep the bullions too neat as they look more realistic if they are different sizes and shapes.

Work the leaves in Q or R, starting with the centre stem of each leaf. With a straight stitch, embroider the soft tops in straight stitch as shown in diagram 4.

earth embroider the earth under the carrots and spade with B in split stitch.

trees using AA, BB and CC, stitch the tree on the left and using A and B the tree on the right with interlocked straight stich for the trunk and straight stitch for the branches.
Work random two wrap French knots and small detached chains in Q, R and S for the left tree leaves. Using 2 strands of U or V, stitch the right tree leaves in horizontal straight stitch.

turnips trace six small circles from the tracing pattern and cut out from white felt. Each turnip requires two small felt circles. Couch them in position with white sewing cotton using small stitches as shown in diagram 5 below. Embroider the turnip starting at the top, covering the felt padding and changing colour down to the tip as shown in diagram 5. As you stitch the edge of the top of the turnip tuck your needle slightly under the felt to give a rounded shape. Keep your sewing tension relaxed. Underline the tip of the turnip with J. Stitch the leaves using cast-on stitch and S, BB and CC. Start each leaf from the centre of the top of the turnip. To finish, embroider four straight stitches over the base of the leaves as shown in diagram 5.

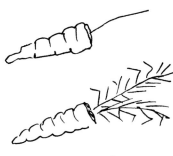

DIAGRAM 4

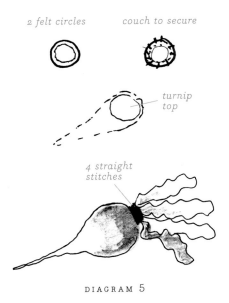

2 felt circles   *couch to secure*

turnip top

4 straight stitches

DIAGRAM 5

carrot bunny

carrot bunny
tracing pattern

*turnips
cut 6
white felt
circles*

stitch direction

carrot bunny
colour location

d.545
d.648
d.646
d.675

d.949

d.093

d.947

d.095

d.949
d.943
d.947
d.991
d.949
d.990

d.406

d.547
d.675
d.677

d.408

d.947
d.943

s.869
s.865
s.867

d.406

d.949
d.947

d.344

d.344

d.545
d.547

d.545
d.547

d.949

d.785
8940

d.545
d.547

d.992

d.947

d.947
d.943
d.949

d.785
8940

d.545
d.547

threads

GUMNUT YARNS 'DAISIES' 1-ply fine wool

A = d.949 ultra dk hazelnut	*head, paws, feet & tree*
B = d.947 dk hazelnut	*head, paws feet, tree & earth*
C = d.943 lt hazelnut	*head, paws, feet & tree*
D = d.991 ecru	*head*
E = d.095 med raspberry	*ears & nose*
F = d.093 lt raspberry	*ears*
G = d.990 white	*collar & turnips*
H = d.408 vy dk sky blue	*jacket*
I = d.406 med dk sky blue	*jacket*
J = d.344 med lt denim	*trousers & turnip outlines*
K = d.992 vy lt pewter	*spade*
L = d.349 ultra dk denim	*outlines*
M = d.785 med apricot delight	*carrots*
N = d.277 dk hyacinth	*turnips*
O = d.275 med hyacinth	*turnips*
P = d.273 lt hyacinth	*turnips*
Q = d.545 med forest grove	*grass, tree leaves & carrot leaves*
R = d.547 dk forest grove	*grass, tree leaves & carrot leaves*
S = d.648 vy dk khaki	*tree & turnip leaves*
T = d.646 med dk khaki	*tree leaves*
U = d.677 dk olive	*tree leaves*
V = d.675 med olive	*tree leaves*

GUMNUT YARNS 'BUDS' perle silk

W = b.949 ultra dk hazelnut	*spade handle*

GUMNUT YARNS 'STARS' stranded silk

X = s.869 ultra dk flesh	*tree*
Y = s.867 dk flesh	*tree*
Z = s.865 med flesh	*tree*

D.M.C. BRODER MÉDICIS 1-ply wool

AA = 8940 orange	*carrots*
BB = 8341 dk green	*turnip leaves*
CC = 8418 lt green	*turnip leaves*

D.M.C. stranded cotton

DD = 310 black	*eyes & mouth*

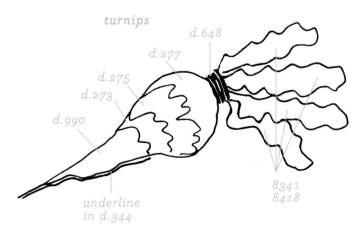

turnips
d.648
d.277
d.275
d.273
d.990
8341
8418
underline in d.344

carrot bunny

barrow bunny
stitch instructions

eye outline the shape of the eye with W using tiny backstitches. Once you have the right shape, fill in the pupil with satin stitch.

nose using E, work three tiny straight stitches on top of each other.

head, ears, paws & feet using interlocked straight stitch and starting with D, embroider around the eye area and then the whisker pads. Change to C and fill out the area just worked, interlocking the stitches so the colour change is gradual and does not have the appearance of stripes. Change to A and embroider the darkest areas of the face and base of the ears. Using B, complete the areas marked, locking the stitches into A and C, giving subtle changes in colour. Work the base of the ears in A and complete the paws and feet referring to the colour and stitch direction charts.

One small straight stitch in A is enough to form the shadows between the toes.

DIAGRAM 1

shirt embroider the braces once the shirt and trousers have been completed. Using P, work the outline of the shirtsleeve in backstitch, leaving the creases in the sleeve until after the sleeve is completed. Continue to fill in the sleeve with I. Add the creases with P as shown in diagram 1.

Embroider the darker areas of the shirt in G and complete in H.

trousers work the trousers in interlocked straight stitch carefully following the colour and stitch direction charts. Stitch the waistband last as this gives a neat finish between the shirt and trousers.

Embroider the lower edge of each trouser cuff and shirt cuff with A in straight stitch as shown in diagram 2.

DIAGRAM 2

barrow
bunny

barrow bunny
stitch instructions [continued]

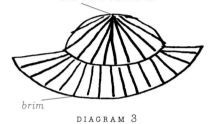

start at the centre of the crown and work outwards

brim

DIAGRAM 3

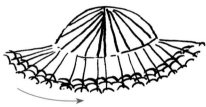

work rows from left to right

DIAGRAM 4

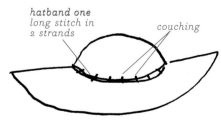

hatband one long stitch in 2 strands

couching

DIAGRAM 5

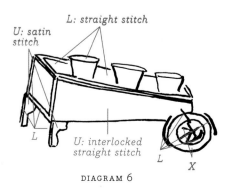

L: straight stitch

U: satin stitch

L

U: interlocked straight stitch

L

X

DIAGRAM 6

hat embroider the hatband once the hat is completed. Using T and raised stem stitch, work the brim and the crown separately. Starting with the crown, work vertical straight stitch from the centre fanning out as shown in diagram 3. Fasten off the thread. Next work vertical straight stitch on the brim. Referring to diagram 3, note that these stitches do not have to be parallel and if the odd one is slightly wider than the other it will give the wicker hat an 'aged' appearance. Continuing with T, work in stem stitch from left to right, wrapping around the vertical threads and being careful not catch the fabric underneath. The stitches should sit on top of the fabric. Once you have come to the end of each row secure the thread by working a tiny straight stitch and then stitching back into itself. Cut the thread and return to the left side and commence another row. Don't pull the thread too tightly as you work, just ease the rows of stem stitch towards the edge of the brim as shown in diagram 4.
Embroider the crown in the same way as the brim. Treat the whole process as if you are weaving.

hatband & braces stitch the hatband in 2 strands of K with one long stitch and couch down at short intervals with H as shown in diagram 5. Embroider the braces over the top of the shirt with T, working two rows of backstitch. Form the leather buttonholes with detached chains. Partially outline the braces with L and form the buttons with two wrap French knots.

barrow & pots work the pots in the barrow with O in satin stitch and then work the barrow following the colour and stitches as shown in diagram 6. For the handles, using V, work two plumb-lines from the rabbit's paws to the barrow. Next lay three more long stitches over the top of these first ones. Keep your stitches straight, but not tight. Continuing with V, couch these stitches down with close even stitches, working from underneath rather than to the side of the plumb-lines. This gives the handles a more rounded appearance.

Embroider the wheel using a no.18 chenille needle and 6 strands of X. Bring the thread to the top of your work and using a second smaller needle and 1 strand of X, couch down the 6 strands into a circular shape as shown in diagram 7. Once you have completed your wheel, take the 6 strands on the larger needle back to the underside of your work by going slightly past your starting point and tuck the needle underneath to form a neat join. Fasten off the threads, finish and secure the couching. Using 1 strand of X and straight stitch, form the wheel spokes. Partially outline and shade the wheel in L, paying close attention to diagram 8 below. Continuing with L, partially outline the handles and legs of the barrow and shade the inside of the barrow.

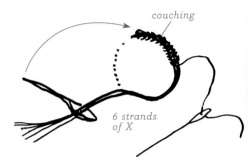

DIAGRAM 7

DIAGRAM 8

flower stems embroider in split stitch with M.

leaves using N, form detached chains and four to five single wrap French knots for the foliage.

flowers stitch the petals with eight or nine detached chains worked in 2 strands of Q, R or S. Work the centres with three wrap French knots in G, secured with a single couching stitch.

grass embroider with M and N together in the needle and horizontal split stitches.

birds using straight stitch, work a wide `M` shape with 2 strands of O for each bird.

tail embroider the tail using D in a small cluster of ghiordes knots. Secure each loop with a tiny straight stitch. Work to a rhythm …stitch, loop, stitch, loop, stitch.
Cut the loops and comb out the threads to form a soft tail.

barrow bunny

barrow bunny
tracing pattern

stitch direction

barrow bunny
colour location

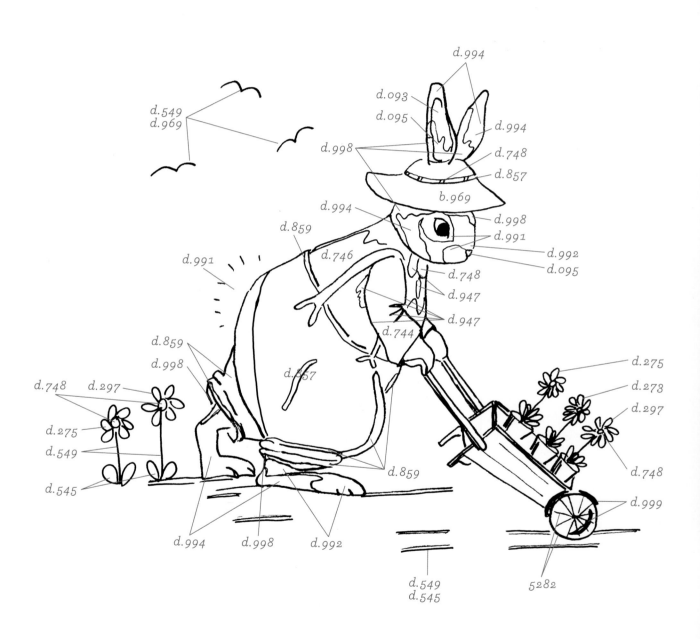

threads

GUMNUT YARNS 'DAISIES' 1-ply fine wool

A = d.998 vy dk pewter — *head, ears, trouser & sleeve cuffs*
B = d.994 med lt pewter — *head, ears, paws & feet*
C = d.992 vy lt pewter — *face, paws & feet*
D = d.991 ecru — *face & tail*
E = d.095 med raspberry — *ears & nose*
F = d.093 lt raspberry — *ears*
G = d.748 vy dk daffodil — *shirt & flower centres*
H = d.746 med dk daffodil — *shirt & hatband*
I = d.744 med lt daffodil — *shirtsleeve*
J = d.859 ultra dk salmon pink — *trousers*
K = d.857 dk salmon pink — *trousers & hatband*
L = d.999 nearly black — *inside barrow & partial outline*
M = d.549 ultra dk forest grove — *flowers stems, grass & birds*
N = d.545 med forest grove — *leaves & grass*
O = d.969 ultra dk chocolate dip — *plant pots & birds*
P = d.947 dk hazelnut — *shading & outline on shirtsleeve*
Q = d.275 med hyacinth — *flowers*
R = d.273 lt hyacinth — *flowers*
S = d.297 dk lavender — *flower*

GUMNUT YARNS 'BUDS' perle silk

T = b.969 ultra dk chocolate dip — *hat & braces*
U = b.967 dk chocolate dip — *barrow*
V = b.945 med hazelnut — *barrow handles*

D.M.C. stranded cotton

W = 310 black — *eye*

D.M.C. stranded metallic thread

X = 5282 gold — *wheel*

> All embroidery is worked with the fabric in a hoop. Use one strand of thread unless otherwise stated.

apple bunny
stitch instructions

eye outline the shape of the eye with U in tiny backstitches and fill in the pupil with satin stitch.

nose fill in with three tiny straight stitches using F, building the stitches up rather than spreading them out.

head, ears, paws, lower body & legs using interlocked straight stitch and starting with E, work the area around the eye. Change to D and stitch just above and below the nose. Work the darker areas in A, following the stitch direction and colour charts. Next work in B adding flecks of lighter colour with D and then complete the face in C. Continue to stitch the ears, paws, lower body and legs in interlocked straight stitch, following the stitch direction and colour charts. Start in the centre of the lower ear and work out. Complete by working the partial outlines on the feet and legs in straight stitch using A.

jacket stitch the darker areas first in H and then complete in I. Work the small stitching on the jacket with 2 strands of U. Do not pull the stitches tightly; place them on top of the blue area already completed. On the jacket back tab work two, triple wrap, French knots for the buttons and couch these to secure. Using tiny backstitches work the pocket. Outline the sleeve and jacket with straight stitches and add the little creases in the right hand sleeve.

tree start with the knothole, stitching as shown in diagram 1.
Add a partial knot further down the trunk. Complete the trunk and branches using O, P and then Q, following the stitch direction and colour charts.

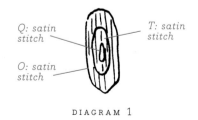

Q: satin stitch
T: satin stitch
O: satin stitch

DIAGRAM 1

apple bunny

leaves using detached chain stitch, embroider each leaf in J, K or L. Work the colours in groups, as this will give a more realistic effect. Keep the darker green to the left side of the tree.

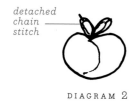

detached chain stitch

DIAGRAM 2

tree apples work in M and N using small interlocked straight stitches. Add leaves to the apples with two detached chains in J or K as shown in diagram 2.

ladder embroider using interlocked straight stitch, refering to the colour and stitch direction charts for stitch placement. Do not allow your stitches to get too long.

apples in string bag trace the apple shape from the tracing pattern and cut out eight circles from red felt. Using two circles for each apple and red sewing cotton and tiny stitches, couch each one in position towards the top of the ladder. Place a second shape over each of the first and couch in place as shown in diagram 3.

Embroider over the felt using M and N. Do not pull the stitches tightly. Allow the thread to cover the felt without pulling it flat. When stitching the edge of each apple, tuck the needle just under the felt to keep the apple well rounded as shown in diagram 4.

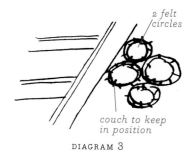

2 felt circles

couch to keep in position

DIAGRAM 3

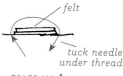

felt

tuck needle under thread

DIAGRAM 4

string bag following diagram 5, start at the ladder edge and, using 2 strands of Q, form a loop and secure with a straight stitch and then stitch back into it. This loop forms the top of the string bag. Changing to a single thread, stitch blanket stitch along the loop, keeping the stitches close together and as even as possible. Next work long loose cross stitches from the top of the bag to underneath the lower apples, securing each stitch. Using A, K or L, add leaves to each of the apples.

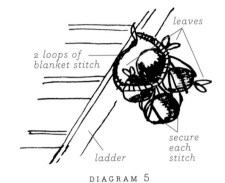

DIAGRAM 5

tail embroider the tail using E in a small cluster of ghiordes knots. Secure each loop with a tiny straight stitch. Work to a rhythm ...stitch, loop, stitch, loop, stitch.
Cut the loops and comb out the threads to form a soft tail.

apple bunny
tracing pattern

Apples in string bag

cut 8 in
red felt

stitch direction

apple bunny
colour location

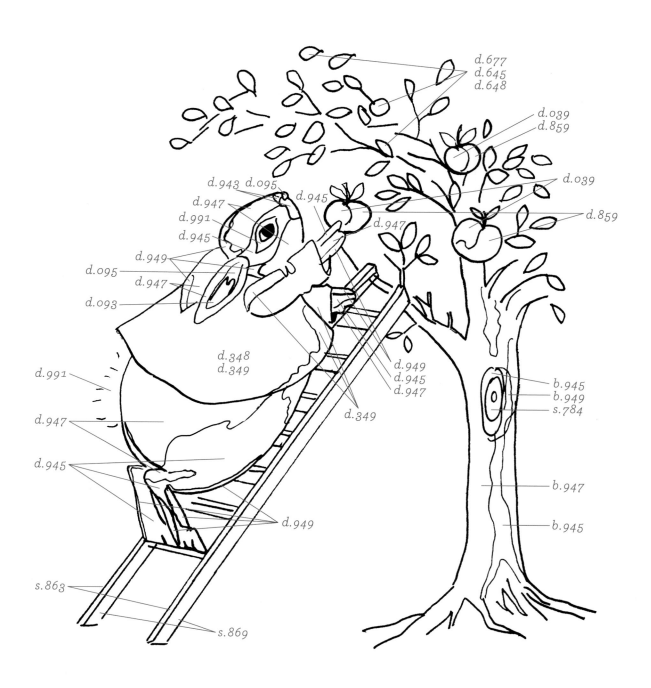

threads

GUMNUT YARNS 'DAISIES' 1-ply fine wool

A = d.949 ultra dk hazelnut   *head, ears, paws, lower body & feet*
B = d.947 dk hazelnut   *head, ears, paws & feet*
C = d.945 med hazelnut   *head, paws, lower body & feet*
D = d.943 lt hazelnut   *head & tummy*
E = d.991 ecru   *head & tail*
F = d.095 med raspberry   *ears & nose*
G = d.093 lt raspberry   *ears*
H = d.349 ultra dk denim   *jacket*
I = d.348 very dk denim   *jacket*
J = d.648 very dk khaki   *leaves*
K = d.645 med khaki   *leaves*
L = d.677 dark olive   *leaves*
M = d.039 ultra dk coral sunset   *apples*
N = d.859 ultra dk salmon pink   *apples*

GUMNUT YARNS 'BUDS' perle silk

O = b.949 ultra dk hazelnut   *tree*
P = b.947 dk hazelnut   *tree*
Q = b.945 med hazelnut   *tree & string bag*

GUMNUT YARNS 'STARS' stranded silk

R = s.869 ultra dk flesh   *ladder*
S = s.863 lt flesh   *ladder*
T = s.784 med light apricot delight   *knot hole in tree trunk*

D.M.C. stranded cotton

U = 310 black   *eye & jacket top stitching*

> All embroidery is worked with the fabric in a hoop. Use one strand of thread unless otherwise stated.

cauliflower bunny
stitch instructions

eyes outline the shape of the full eye with V in tiny backstitches to obtain the right size and shape. Once you are happy with the shape fill in with satin stitch. The rabbit's partial eye is two small straight stitches. As the rabbit is too small to work individual eye lashes, the suggestion of eyelashes is achieved by working a single straight stitch at the top of each eye.

mouth stitch the mouth and underside of the nose in V with tiny straight stitches.

nose embroider two or three tiny straight stitches in E. To avoid the nose becoming too large, work these stitches on top of each other.

head, ears, paws & feet using D and interlocked straight stitch, embroider around the eye area and the whisker pads. Change to A and work the darker areas on the base of the ears, back of the head and under the chin. Remember to keep the stitches flowing in the right direction. Complete the rest of the face, ears, paws and feet, carefully following the stitch direction and colour charts. Partially outline the paws and feet in A.

jacket embroider the buttons in 2 strands of V in triple wrap French knots and couch to secure. Work shading at the jacket cuffs with V as shown in diagram 1.

DIAGRAM 1

trousers stitch the trousers, carefully following the stitch direction and colour charts and then partially outline in broken straight stitch in B.

tail embroider the tail using D in a small cluster of ghiordes knots.
Secure each loop with a tiny straight stitch. Work to a rhythm …stitch, loop, stitch, loop, stitch.
Cut the loops and comb out the threads to form a soft tail.

cauliflower
bunny

cauliflower bunny
stitch instructions [continued]

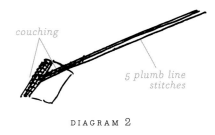

couching

5 plumb line stitches

DIAGRAM 2

hoe using T, work a plumb-line from the ground to between the rabbits paws and then a second plumb-line from under the rabbit's arm to form the end of the hoe handle. These lines should be straight but not tight. Now lay four more stitches as close as possible to each other. Secure the thread as shown in diagram 2. Couch the five strands with small even stitches. Bring the needle up from underneath the stitches when working the couching and take the needle down by tucking it under the plumb-lines. This forms a more rounded appearance rather than a flat looking handle.

The end of the hoe is worked in the same manner by laying down plumb-lines and then couching them down as shown in diagram 2.

Embroider the blade with N in satin stitch and then outline with S using straight stitch.

earth embroider in interlocked straight stitch and straight stitch in R.

cauliflower heads stitch three or four wrap French knots in G and C. Keep the knots very close together to form tight cauliflower heads. Embroider the leaves in P and Q using cast-on stitch. Work around each cauliflower head and layer the leaves as shown in diagram 3. Keep most of the leaves at the base of the cauliflower head to give the appearance of the cauliflower lying slightly on its side.

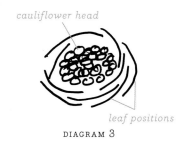

cauliflower head

leaf positions

DIAGRAM 3

basket work three plumb-lines for the sides and base of the basket in U. Secure the thread after each stitch to hold the lines in position as shown in diagram 4.

Remember to keep these lines straight but not tight.

Embroider vertical straight stitches as shown in diagram 5.

Secure each thread with a tiny straight stitch and then stitch back onto itself. Working from left to right, stitch rows of raised stem stitch along the vertical threads. Do not catch the fabric behind. At the end of each row secure the thread as before. To keep the basket in shape, before you start the next row, secure the thread to the left of the first vertical thread as shown in diagram 6.

Work two loops at each side of the basket for the handles and couch with small even stitches. Embroider a cauliflower in the basket. Using A, outline the lower part of the basket and the ground and fill in any gaps at the top of the basket with straight stitch.

birds embroider the birds O in straight stitch in a wide 'M' shape. Add extra stitches to form the thicker part of the wings.

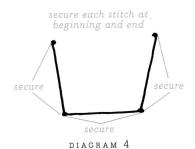

secure each stitch at beginning and end

secure   *secure*

secure

DIAGRAM 4

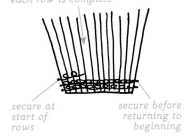

secure stitches

DIAGRAM 5

ease stitches downward when each row is complete

secure at start of rows   *secure before returning to beginning*

DIAGRAM 6

cauliflower bunny
tracing pattern

stitch direction

cauliflower bunny
colour location

d.947
d.991
d.095
d.949
d.093
d.388
d.947
d.991
d.943
d.998
d.648
d.943
d.646
d.646
d.646
d.990
d.646
d.645
d.943
d.991
d.947
d.645
310
310
d.648
d.648
d.746
d.746
d.587
d.589
d.994
d.746
d.748
d.746
d.744
d.748
d.947
d.587
d.589
d.990
d.943
d.949
d.990
d.943
d.966

threads

....

GUMNUT YARNS 'DAISIES' 1-ply fine wool

A = d.949 ultra dk hazelnut	*head, paws, feet, basket, belt & outlines*
B = d.947 dk hazelnut	*head, paws & feet*
C = d.943 lt hazelnut	*head, ears & cauliflower*
D = d.991 ecru	*head, ears & tail*
E = d.095 med raspberry	*ears & nose*
F = d.093 lt raspberry	*ears*
G = d.990 white	*collar, shirt & cauliflower*
H = d.648 vy dk khaki	*jacket & pocket*
I = d.646 med dk khaki	*jacket*
J = d.645 med khaki	*jacket sleeve*
K = d.748 vy dk daffodil	*trousers*
L = d.746 med dk daffodil	*trousers*
M = d.744 med lt daffodil	*trousers*
N = d.994 med lt pewter	*hoe*
O = d.388 vy dk cornflower	*birds*
P = d.589 ultra dk apple green	*cauliflower leaves*
Q = d.587 dk apple green	*cauliflower leaves*
R = d.966 med dk chocolate dip	*earth*
S = d.998 vy dk pewter	*hoe outlines*

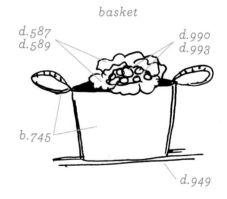

basket

d.587
d.589

d.990
d.993

b.745

d.949

GUMNUT YARNS 'BUDS' perle silk

T = b.949 ultra dk hazelnut	*hoe handle*
U = b. 945 med hazelnut	*basket*

D.M.C. stranded cotton

V = 310 black	*eyes, mouth, buttons, pocket lining & cuffs*

autumn bunny
stitch instructions

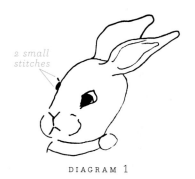

2 small stitches

DIAGRAM 1

eyes outline the full eye with Q in tiny backstitches following the tracing pattern to obtain the correct size and shape. Fill in the pupil with satin stitch. Embroider one small straight stitch for the partial eye, then one tiny straight stitch to give the illusion of eyelashes as shown in diagram 1.

mouth continuing with Q, embroider the mouth and the underside of the nose with small straight stitches.

nose fill in with two or three small straight stitches, placing the stitches on top of each other rather than laying them side-by-side.

head, ears, paws & feet embroider D around the eye area following the stitch direction chart, then work the whisker pads and chin using interlocked straight stitch. Change to A and stitch from the top of the nose up towards the forehead then two or three stitches behind the lower ear. Continue to fill in the head following the colour and stitch direction charts.

ghiordes knots

couching stitches

DIAGRAM 2

scarf using G, stitch the scarfe in interlocked stem stitch, adding the fringe on each end in ghiordes knots. Couch them down in the same thread so as to keep them flat and trim the loops as shown in diagram 2.

jacket work in interlocked straight stitch, filling in the darker areas with I. Continue to fill in the jacket with H and edge in small split stitches using G. Embroider the little buttons with two wrap French knots in H, securing each with a small couching stitch.

autumn
bunny

autumn bunny
stitch instructions [continued]

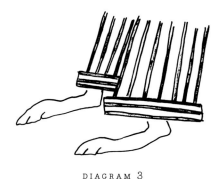

DIAGRAM 3

trousers using interlocked straight stitch, start with the darker coloured stripes reducing the width of the stripes as you get closer to the feet. Do not try to work complete stripes or to match the exact width on every one as it looks unnatural as shown in diagram 3.

Pay close attention to someone wearing a striped shirt or dress and you will see some of the stripes disappear in the natural creases of the fabric.

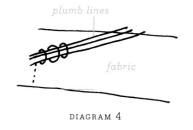

DIAGRAM 4

rake using O, stitch a plumb-line handle from the ground to the bunny's underarm and continue with a short stitch on the other side of his arm. Do not pull these stitches too tight. Next work three more stitches in the same way on top of each other. Carefully couch over the top of these stitches keeping your couching stitches close together as shown in diagram 4. Bring the needle up from under the plumb-lines and cross over them. Take the needle back down in almost the same position as you came up under the plumb-line.

This gives the rake handle a round look like a pole, not a flat stick.

Continue with O and embroider the rake fingers with four straight stitches. Add one angled stitch on each finger to complete.

DIAGRAM 5

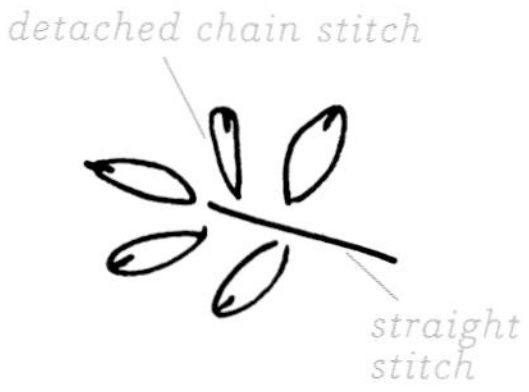

tree work the tree trunk in interlocked straight stitch using O and P. Embroider the branches in straight stitch, following the colour chart for colour changes.

autumn leaves using B, L, M and N, stitch a straight stitch and then add five detached chains as shown in diagram 5 for each autumn leaf.

tracing pattern

autumn bunny
colour location

d.947

d.093

d.095

d.949

d.991

d.943

d.468

d.197

b.967

d.947

d.195

d.468

d.943

b.945

b.967

d.199

d.466

d.945

d.947

d.943

threads

GUMNUT YARNS 'DAISIES' 1-ply fine wool

A = d. 949 ultra dk hazelnut — *head, ears, paws & feet*
B = d. 947 dk hazelnut — *head, ears, paws, feet & leaves*
C = d. 943 lt hazelnut — *head, ears, paws & feet*
D = d. 991 ecru — *head*
E = d. 095 med raspberry — *ears & nose*
F = d. 093 lt raspberry — *ears*
G = d. 468 vy dk sea spray — *scarf, jacket piping & trousers*
H = d. 466 med dk sea spray — *stripes on trousers & buttons*
I = d. 197 dk ripe plum — *jacket*
J = d. 195 med ripe plum — *jacket*
K = d. 199 ultra dk ripe plum — *stripes on trousers*
L = d. 785 med apricot delight — *leaves*
M = d. 827 dk peach melba — *leaves*
N = d. 748 vy dk daffodil — *leaves*

GUMNUT YARNS 'BUDS' perle silk

O = b. 967 dk chocolate dip — *tree & rake*
P = b. 945 med hazelnut — *tree*

D.M.C. stranded cotton

Q = 310 black — *eyes, mouth & nose*

> All embroidery is worked with the fabric in a hoop. Use one strand of thread unless otherwise stated.

autumn bunny
stitch direction

thread painting

stitch glossary

stitch glossary

backstitch

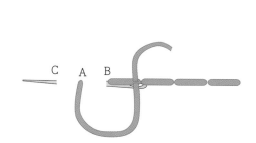 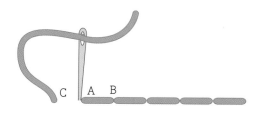

blanket stitch

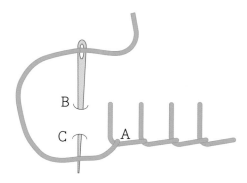

bullion knot

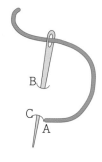 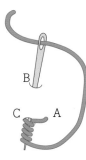 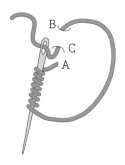

cast-on stitch

- Bring thread to the front of the work at A, insert the needle at B a short distance from A and leave the needle in the fabric.
- Slide your left index finger under the emerging thread.
  Twist your finger around and towards the left to form a loop.

- Place the tip of your left index finger on the tip of the needle.
- Slide the formed loop onto the needle and pull gently so that the loop slides along the needle back towards A.

This forms your first cast-on stitch.

- Hold the cast-on loops with your left index finger and thumb and with your right hand pull the needle through the stitches.
- Take the needle to the back of the fabric at B and secure.
- Repeat until desired number of cast on loops have been created.

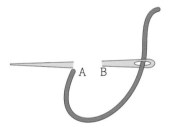

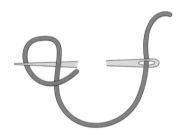

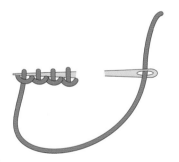

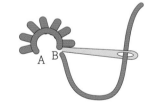

stitch glossary

couching

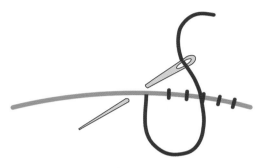

cross stitch

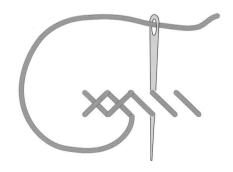

detached chain

fly stitch

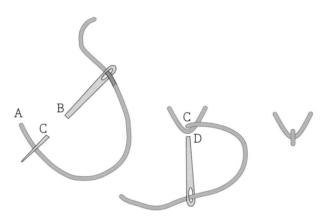

french knot

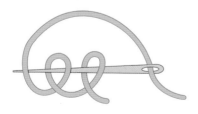

stitch glossary

ghiordes knot

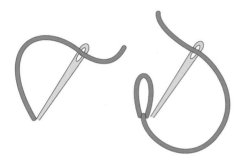  

- Form a loop.
- Work a tiny straight stitch at the base of the loop.
- Form another loop.
- Again secure at the base with a tiny stitch.

Continue in this manner until you have covered the required area.

- Cut the loops and trim to the desired length or shape.

If you intend to trim the loops it is advisable to make them a little longer than required. If you are not cutting the loops, as when working Bumblebee wings for example, make the loops the correct size as you stitch.

interlocked straight stitch

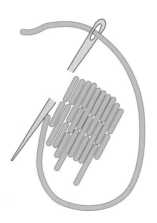

palestrina stitch

- Bring the needle up at A. Take the needle back down approx. 4mm ($3/16''$) away at B.
- Bring the needle to the left at C and pull the thread through.
- Slide the needle under the first stitch from right to left. Do not pierce the fabric.

- Pull the thread through. Do not pull the thread tightly, just allow the thread to gently wrap the straight stitch.
- Allow the thread to form a loop to the left and then, without catching the fabric, slide the needle between B and C, making sure the needle

tip glides over the top of the loop.
- Repeat steps to form the first knot. To create the second knot repeat steps, working to the desired length of stitching.

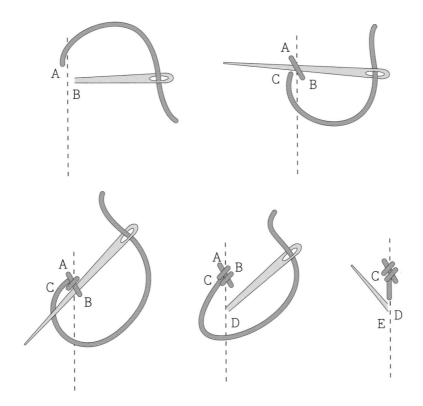

stitch glossary

raised stem stitch

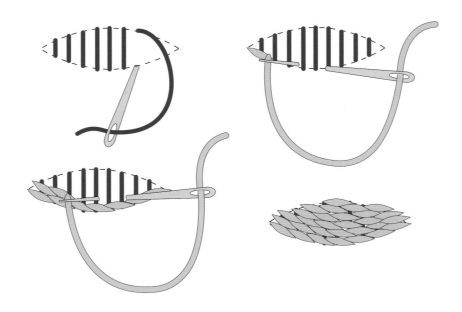

satin stitch

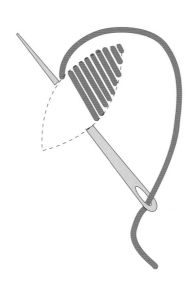

split stitch

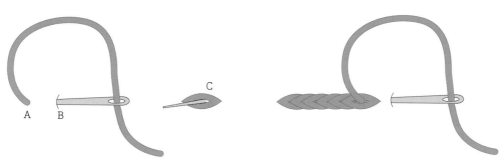

stem stitch

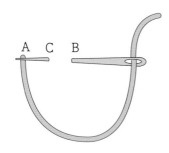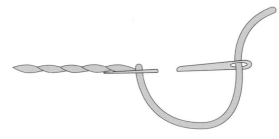

straight stitch

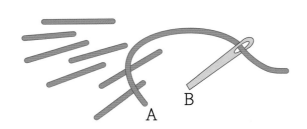

suppliers

Jenny McWhinney Designs

tel: +61 (0)8 8377 0471

email:jennymcw@esc.net.au

web: http://www.jennymcwhinneydesigns.com

GUMNUT YARNS

Australia

PO Box 519

Mudgee NSW 2850 Australia

tel: +61 (0)2 6374 2661

fax: +61 (0)2 6374 2771

email:info@gumnutyarns.com

web: http://www.gumnutyarns.com

USA

Custom House of Needle Art

LLC 154 Weir Street

Glastonburg CT 06033 U.S.A

tel /fax: 860 633 2950

DMC

Australia

Radda Pty Ltd

51-55 Carrington Rd,

Marrickville NSW 2204 Australia

USA

The DMC Corporation

10 Port Kearny

South Kearny NJ 07039

tel : 1 973 589 0606

U.K

D.M.C Creative World Ltd

Pullman Rd, Wigston

Leicestershire LE18 2DY

tel : 44 116 281 1040

South Africa

D.M.C Creative World (Pty) Ltd.

Hill's Building's

Buchanan Square

162 Sir Lowry Rd

8001 Cape Town

South Africa

tel : 27 21 161 9482